MW01613625

Shopping
Is Better Than
Therapy

ROXANNE A. UYEDA

Illustrated and Designed by
Lianne U. Liang

ATSUKO
PUBLISHING

• Shopping Is Better Than Therapy •

ROXANNE A. UYEDA

Contributors:
Kim R. West, Laura B. Thibodeaux, Elina Green

Illustration and Design:
Lianne U. Liang,
Liang Publication & Production Services

昼子

ATSUKO PUBLISHING
8116 Arlington Boulevard, Suite 164
Falls Church, Virginia 22042
www.atsukopublish.com

FIRST EDITION

Shopping Is Better Than Therapy™ 1998

ISBN 0-9665467-0-9
Library of Congress Catalog Card Number 98-93229

If you would like to share any thoughts about this book or
are interested in other books and products by Atsuko Publishing,
please write to our address above.

Several months ago, I was talking to two friends and we landed on the subject of shopping. This topic began with how we deal with every day life (e.g., heartbreak, husbands, divorces, running a business, stress in the office, kids) and what we do to either reward ourselves for having to deal with it, or how we escape it...
We realized that...well...we go shopping.

This book is comprised of some of those rather whimsical and fun thoughts that we had that day as well as several quotes from other friends (who all agreed that going shopping can indeed, often feel better than therapy.)

Happy reading for you avid shoppers and hope you have as much fun with this enlightening thought as we did!

. . . .

Thank you for your help, insightfulness and humor:

Kim R. West
Laura B. Thibodeaux
Elina Green

Thank you to my sister, Lianne U. Liang (President, Liang Publication and Production Services) for supporting me, encouraging me and going the extra several miles to help me put this book together.

Thank you to those of you who provided me with your thoughts but choose to remain anonymous (you know who you are!)

. . . .

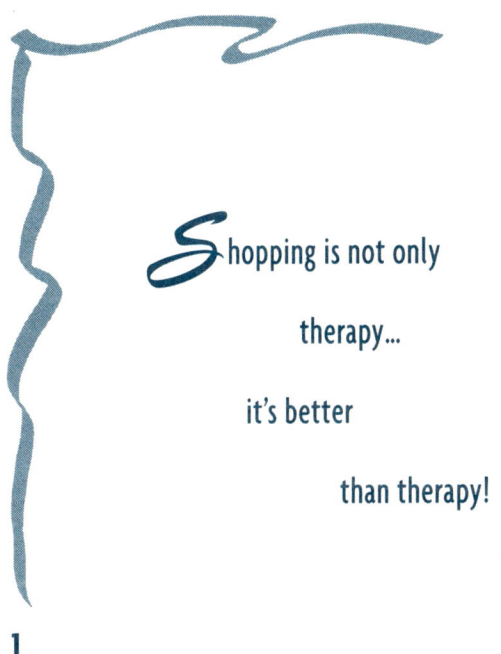

*S*hopping is not only

therapy...

it's better

than therapy!

1

$\mathcal{M}$y colleague and friend in New Orleans developed a theory that some people might be better off taking their $75.00 (or more) to shop instead of going to therapy (this excludes the murderers and other "bringers" of serious mayhem of course!!)

2

—BY LAURA B. THIBODEAUX

*N*irvana is the smell of

     new paper and fresh ink,

the quiet rustling of readers,

  soft meditative music

     in my head, and six

  new books in my shopping bag.

—BY KIM R. WEST

3

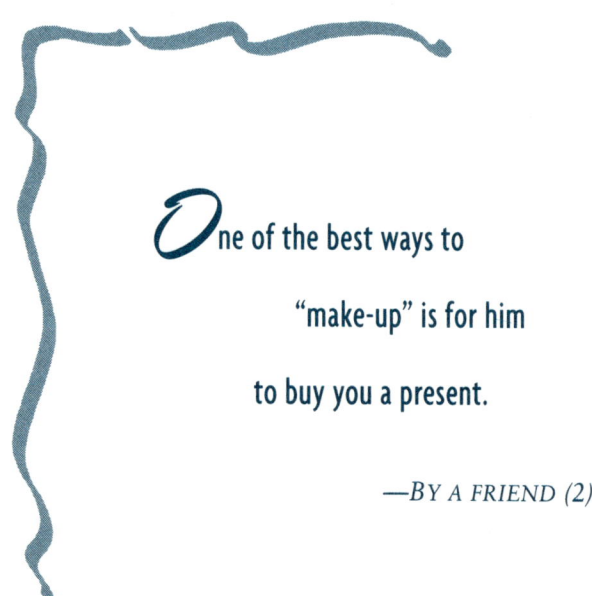

*O*ne of the best ways to

"make-up" is for him

to buy you a present.

—*BY A FRIEND (2)*

4

$\mathcal{S}$ay I'm sorry

with a shopping spree.

—BY ELINA GREEN

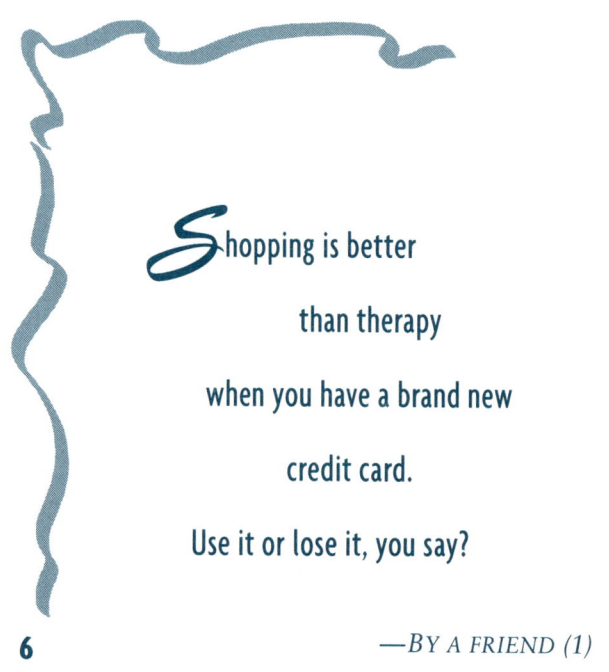

$\mathcal{S}$hopping is better

than therapy

when you have a brand new

credit card.

Use it or lose it, you say?

—*BY A FRIEND (1)*

*S*hopping is contagious ...

If I shop with a friend or two,

it is guaranteed, that

if one of us begins buying,

then all of us begin buying!

—*BY A FRIEND (2)*

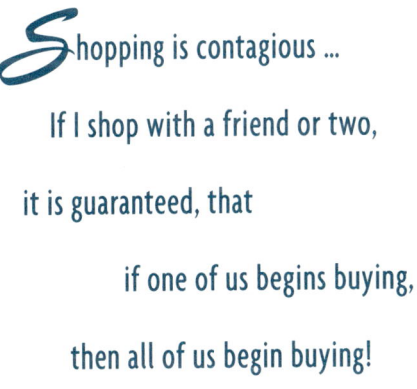

I know my day has been

well ... *spent* ... when my purse

bulges with rustling receipts

and the weight of loose change.

—*BY KIM R. WEST*

8

I don't know what is better, the

shopping networks or catalogs ...

It's just so easy to shop ...

Used to be that you

would have to work for it ... .

—*BY A FRIEND (2)*

$\mathcal{T}$o chase the blues away -

take your catalogues out and play!!!

You can pick and choose all day!!

And order when you're ready to pay!!

—BY LAURA B. THIBODEAUX

10

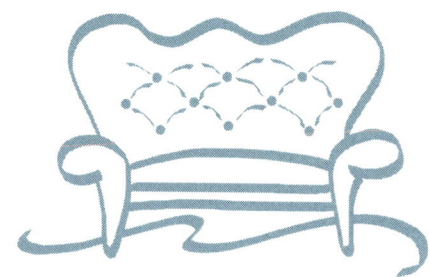

*S*hopping

is the

ultimate

distraction.

$\mathcal{J}$f you want to just decompress, put aside some time away from stresses and take a day to window shop. Weave in and out of stores, make a list of what you would like to buy someday and treat yourself to a nice lunch.

*S*ome stores are a "six sense" experience. You walk in, it smells good, music is playing, good vibes are about!! You can walk around or sit down - take a load off!! I love these kinds of stores.

—*By Laura B. Thibodeaux*

13

*S*hopping is a

delightful experience —

seeing, touching, tasting,

smelling, hearing - all of the senses

are essential.

—*By Kim R. West*

14

*O*nce I was on a long weekend trip with a friend and her mother. Both of their husbands were with us as well. On our trip back, we split up. The men took one car back and we took another. We let them leave first and we trailed, taking the long way back stopping at all of the outlet malls. When we got home, the guys asked us what took us so long ... we responded "we were out spending quality time together."

15

I like to plan my shopping forays.

First is a day of window-shopping

and list-making. Then, I categorize

and prioritize. Then, I buy it all.

—*By Kim R. West*

16

*I*gnore those who try

to discourage you ... ..

go shopping and spend more

than you planned.

—*BY ELINA GREEN*

*D*o you know how to negotiate as you shop?? I actually negotiated the price down on two hats, in the mall (of all places), the other week. Lots of people haggle just for the fun of it. It's a lost art, and sometimes (with empowered sales persons and retail management) you can drum up a bargain. These are good skills to develop anyway, so why not give it a shot?

—*BY LAURA B. THIBODEAUX*

I never wear

a watch

when I shop.

—*By Kim R. West*

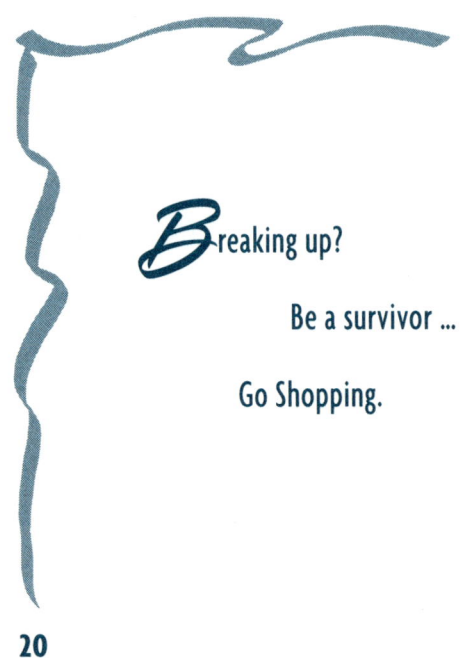

*B*reaking up?

Be a survivor ...

Go Shopping.

20

*P*eople have told me that

a shopping "high" is only

temporary and doesn't make

anything better ...

they must not shop

enough to know better.

I love jade. Whenever I see

jade jewelry, I always

get a craving

for hard candy.

—*BY KIM R. WEST*

22

J "Holiday" shop

all year around.

$\mathcal{I}$f you can't go anywhere

without your children

bugging you for something

everywhere you go,

leave them at home!

24

—*BY THE WORDS OF A CHILD*

*I*nvest in your image -

go shopping!

—*BY ELINA GREEN*

*K*eep a gift drawer. That way when you see something that is perfect for someone (or "someones") you love, you can buy it and save it in the gift drawer for that special occasion.

26

I lie in bed.

I stare at the ceiling.

The clock ticks slowly.

I start to sweat.

Only seven hours until

that sale commences.

—BY KIM R. WEST

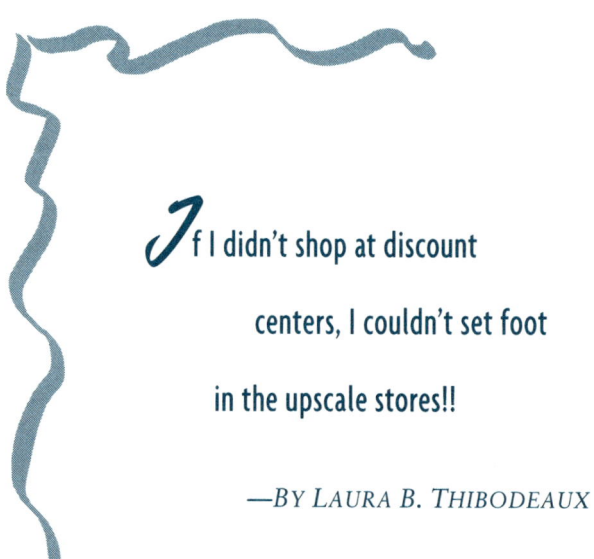

*J*f I didn't shop at discount

centers, I couldn't set foot

in the upscale stores!!

—*BY LAURA B. THIBODEAUX*

28

*F*eeling great is

going to the "dollar" store.

There's NOTHING there

you can't afford!

—*BY A FRIEND (1)*

$\mathcal{G}$oing shopping is

giving yourself

a warm fuzzy.

—BY KIM R. WEST

30

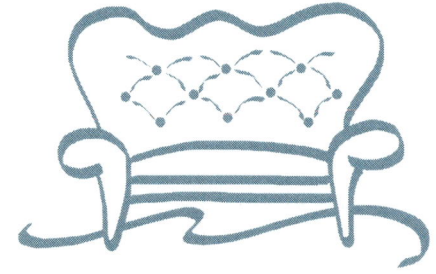

*S*hopping is better than therapy

when you usually have trouble

finding shoes in your size.

Today, you find a great pump

in three fabulous colors.

You take all three!!

—*BY A FRIEND (1)*

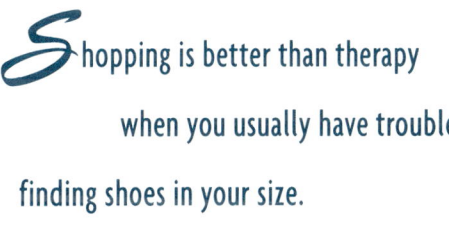

$\mathcal{O}$utlet malls are perfect

for taking a break during

a long road trip.

32

I like to have a reason for shopping:

Easter, birthdays, fun, Christmas, fun,

President's Day, Thanksgiving, fall

equinox, fun, solar eclipse,

Saturday.... oh, did I mention fun?

—*BY KIM R. WEST*

33

Shopping for gift souvenirs

and postcards is one of the

best ways to let people know

you were thinking about them

when you were gone.

*S*ave for a rainy day ...

and then when that

rainy day comes,

go shopping!

There are some of us who feel very generous when we shop. I often follow the "one for them - one for me rule." I love this rule. I love to give gifts, I love to give to me too!!!

I have no guilt, because I bought for others ... I feel like its Christmas because I bought for me too!!!

—BY LAURA B. THIBODEAUX

*S*hopping often

results in giving.

$\mathcal{I}$ keep small gifts handy for the kids for good grades and good behavior, and I love to shop for these things. We all get the rewards. They do for being great kids, and I do from buying the gifts with them in mind.

38

—*BY KIM R. WEST*

*T*o buy something for

someone who has everything

– take them shopping

—*BY ELINA GREEN*

$\mathcal{I}$ love shopping for others and my favorite time is during the holidays. Buying toys for Toys-For-Tots or buying groceries so that other families can enjoy a holiday meal is something I must do to make my holidays complete. I know that I am helping others to enjoy the holidays as much as I do.

40

*W*indow shopping

is guilt free.

*W*hen you compare shopping to therapy ... both can make you feel great ... but consider this ... Buy something and you can have it forever. Get advice on how to be a better you and it might not last the day.

42

—*BY A FRIEND (2)*

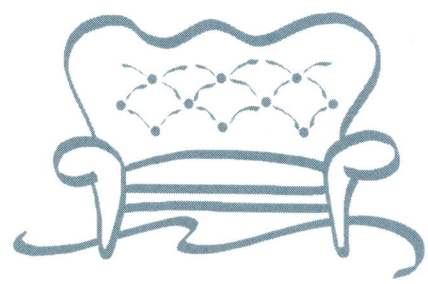

*S*hopping is better than therapy when your kid is begging you for a new sweat suit for next week's school outing. You finally give in to buy it. You get to the cashier and find out it's half price!!!

BY A FRIEND (1)

43

*E*aster is one of my favorite

holidays — shopping for

new dresses, new bonnets,

new shoes, new gloves and candy!

—*BY KIM R. WEST*

44

*S*hopping is better than therapy

when you've waited 'til Christmas

eve to buy your best friend's

present. You know what you want

to get. You get to the store, and it's

there! You get the last one!!!

—*BY A FRIEND (1)*

*R*oadside craft and American Indian

markets in the southwest are

the most fun because you

not only find interesting gifts

but you learn bits and pieces of

American Culture as well.

*B*outiques are another shopping treasure. Boutiques usually carry more unusual or eclectic items that are not likely to be found in mainstream stores. They often are more willing to negotiate prices too!!

—*BY LAURA B. THIBODEAUX*

47

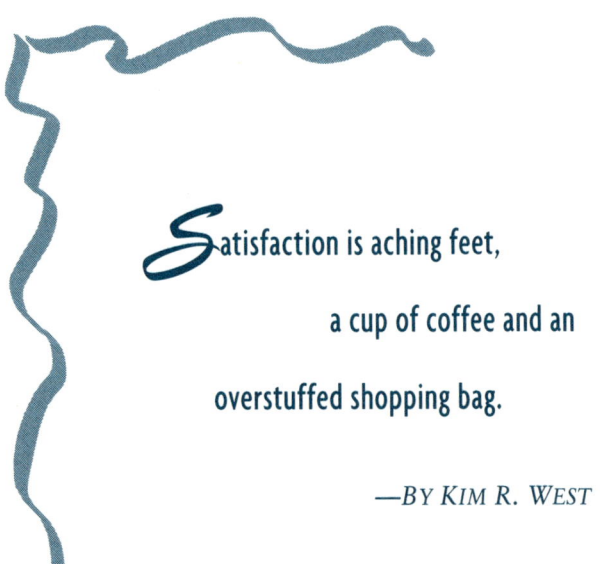

*S*atisfaction is aching feet,

a cup of coffee and an

overstuffed shopping bag.

—*BY KIM R. WEST*

48

*B*uying fresh flowers is always an uplifting thing to do. When I need a little pick-me-up, I love walking into floral shops and having my senses filled with a gentle barrage of scents and colors.

49

—*BY A FRIEND (2)*

*W*hy wait for someone else

to give them? I buy

flowers for myself.

—*BY KIM R. WEST*

50

*D*o you think you are spending too much money in the mall?? Feeling like you're sinking too much into looking good and feeling fine??!!! Well, call your stock broker and buy part of the companies you shop in!!!

—*BY LAURA B. THIBODEAUX*

51

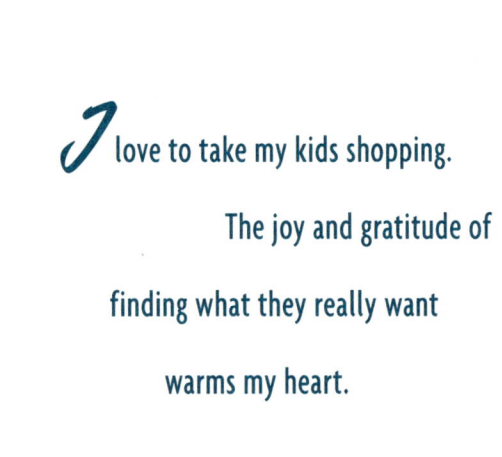

$\mathcal{I}$ love to take my kids shopping.

The joy and gratitude of

finding what they really want

warms my heart.

—*BY KIM R. WEST*

52

I look forward to rainy days

and sunny malls.

—BY KIM R. WEST

*F*eeling great is

splurging for

the good stuff.

54

Shopping patterns are affected

by significant-other relationships

... when you are enamored with

someone special, you want to

shower *that person* with gifts

 ... when you are angry with

that person, you want to shower

yourself with gifts.

A good day of shopping should

be rewarded with a nice meal out

or a Sinfully Delicious Chocolate

Mocha 7-Layer Torte of Delight.

—*BY KIM R. WEST*

*S*hopping is educational!

I love jewelry. I shop for jewelry so

much that I know more about gem

stones then most sales people ...

—*BY A FRIEND (2)*

One time I went into a large discount store to get out of the rain. I had on really high heels with my suit that day. It was raining very hard. You could hear it pounding on the roof. I walked around so long I thought my feet would come apart, when I spotted a pair of cartoon character house slippers. What did I do? I cut off the plastic "doo-hickey" and slipped them on. That's what I did! I carried the tag to the register to pay for them. Did they mind? Nope. Other shoppers thought they were so cute, that the store sold several more pairs that night.

—BY LAURA B. THIBODEAUX

59

*F*eeling great is

getting a

real bargain.

If you understand a single

person purchasing two packs

of 250 count napkins for $1.97,

standup and shout!

—*By Laura B. Thibodeaux*

60

*W*onder is finding that dress

that was in your dream.

—*BY KIM R. WEST*

$\mathcal{I}$ have a friend who argues with her significant other, every time she spends money on something special (but perhaps frivolous) on herself. She discovered that when she brings something home for him too, he doesn't seem to get quite as angry. After all how can you be angry with someone bearing gifts?

*S*hopping is a way to reward

yourself when you've been

good and running from yourself

when you've been bad.

—*BY A FRIEND (2)*

$\mathcal{S}$hopping is a way to

celebrate life's successes.

I think shopping in modern times is like hunting in the ancient days. The thrill of the chase (finding that elusive item), the challenge of testing your skills against the elements (maneuvering through obstacles, crowds and snarly sales clerks), and the gratification of the kill (knowing that one more day of survival has been assured.)

—BY KIM R. WEST

65

*W*ant to impress her

on your first date?

Take her shopping!

—*By Elina Green*

66

Shopping (and window shopping)
can be therapeutic in multiple ways
... not only do you get a mental
break from your problems BUT you
also get EXERCISE ... which WE ALL
know is good for the mind and the
soul. So put on your walking shoes,
select a large shopping mall and
walk 'til you drop!

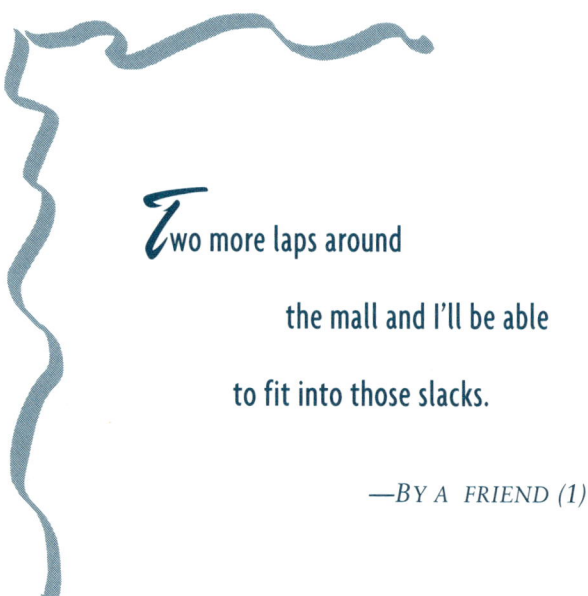

$\mathcal{T}$wo more laps around

the mall and I'll be able

to fit into those slacks.

—*BY A FRIEND (1)*

68

*L*ife is like a mall ... so many

directions to go in and

so many decisions to make.

—*BY KIM R. WEST*

*N*urture Yourself!! Want to treat yourself, but kinda broke?? Well, remember the dollar stores, they have cute underwear, smell goods, pretty vases, wine glasses - and more. Many inspirational stores have pencils, pens, book marks, key chains with inspirational sayings for about $1.00 to $3.50. Also, if available they have free newly released singles of inspirational music that they give away, which can be gifts to yourself or others.

—BY LAURA B. THIBODEAUX

*S*hopping is better than therapy when your child's coat costs twice as much as you expected. A cheaper one would do, but this one looks perfect and the little one really loves it. You decide to wait 'til next month to buy yourself that new exercise equipment you've had your eye on.

—BY A FRIEND (1)

*W*hy do shoppers get so

grumpy during the holiday rush?

Don't they know that

shopping is FUN???

72

*W*hen is the last time you looked for a gift or interesting doo-dad in the grocery store? The supermarket chains usually carry pretty mugs, flower arrangements and potpourri. Some have their own merchandising such as T-shirts, sweatshirts and canvas bags. Next time you forgot someone's birthday or need to cheer yourself up, look for it when you swing by the grocery to get that butter or bottle of wine!!!

—BY LAURA B. THIBODEAUX

73

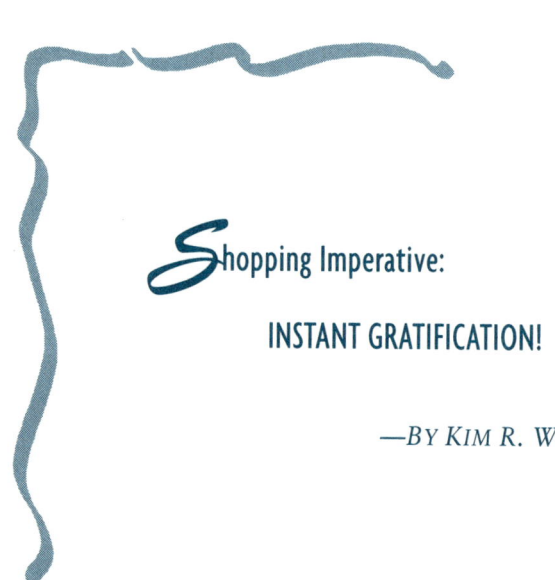

*S*hopping Imperative:

INSTANT GRATIFICATION!

—*By Kim R. West*

*S*hopping is better than therapy

when I find unopened packages

I purchased more than a year ago

and it feels like my birthday

all over again!

—*BY A FRIEND (1)*

Sometimes I can't sleep because

I am thinking of office problems ...

I get my mind off of them by

turning on a network shopping show

and shop until I literally drop

(asleep that is ... .)

*O*ne of the prettiest places

in the U.S. to shop is Carmel, CA.

Every time I go to visit, I weave in

and out of all of the shops and

then when it is time for a break,

I walk down to the beach and

watch the pristine Pacific Ocean.

By the end of the day, I feel

incredibly relaxed and happy.

—*BY A FRIEND (2)*

*H*ave you ever bought anything second hand or antique? This can be a wonderful way to get great treasures at a bargain. Check out an antique store. Some are way over priced, but some have beautiful paintings, vases, china and so on for very reasonable prices. What's more they will often negotiate the price. Beautiful clothes, shoes and jewelry are often sold on consignment - check it out!!!

—*BY LAURA B. THIBODEAUX*

*M*y day is made when I have

looked all over for that

one item (which is the only thing

my father asks for his birthday)

and I finally find it.

My feats of coordination are amazing! Five overstuffed bags, three boxes, my purse and my credit card in my hands, and I can still find the steps with my toes!

—*BY KIM R. WEST*

*W*hat is it about shopping that makes

you feel great? It doesn't solve

problems, it doesn't make you richer,

it doesn't make Mr. (or Ms.) Right fall

in love with you ... It just feels good.

$\mathcal{S}$hopping is like going

on a treasure hunt.

—*BY KIM R. WEST*

*H*e loves another woman.

HE is not worth crying over.

SHE is not worth hating.

Why don't you go shopping instead?

*S*ome people (you know who you are) claim not to like to shop, but when they get near cars, trucks or large home entertainment systems, they forget that "they don't like to shop." These are the BIG TICKET ITEM shoppers!! Their eyes get glazed over by new technology gadgets, power tools, motorcycles, computers and more!!!

—*BY LAURA B. THIBODEAUX*

84

*P*lease don't get me wrong ...

I think therapy is a really really

good thing for people, it's just

that I prefer to shop.

—*BY A FRIEND (2)*

I have been told that one of the

benefits I have being single

is I can buy when I want to,

how I want to and

what I want to.

*T*he epitome of being single:

Going shopping with your

friends on "date night".

—*BY A FRIEND (2)*

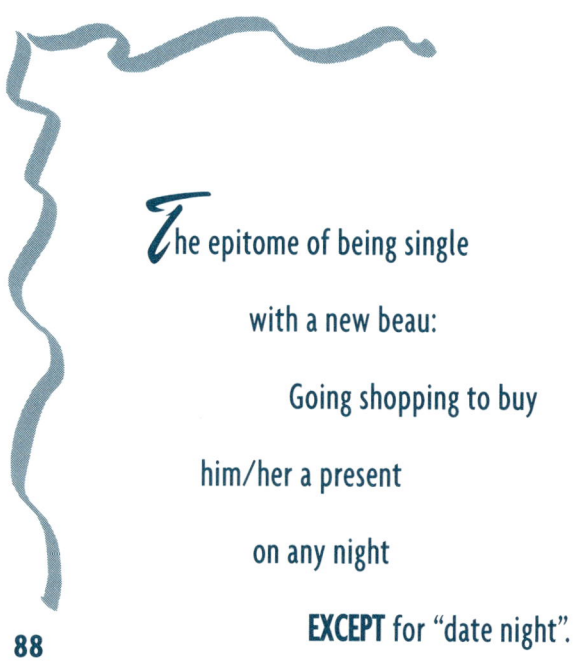

$\mathcal{T}$he epitome of being single

with a new beau:

Going shopping to buy

him/her a present

on any night

EXCEPT for "date night".

88

—BY A FRIEND (2)

*T*he epitome of being free:

Going shopping on a Saturday

morning instead of taking care

of your weekly chores.

—*BY A FRIEND (2)*

$\mathcal{T}$he epitome of being a grandparent:

Going shopping at a toy store

and buying gifts for

the grandchildren.

—*BY A FRIEND (2)*

90

The epitome of being a parent:

Finding a way to buy

something extra for the children

even when it may

not be what they need.

—BY A FRIEND (2)